Two Centuries
of Bach

Da Capo Press Music Reprint Series

MUSIC EDITOR
BEA FRIEDLAND
Ph.D., City University of New York

This title was recommended for Da Capo reprint by
Frank D'Accone, *University of California at Los Angeles*

Two Centuries of Bach

AN ACCOUNT OF CHANGING TASTE

By

FRIEDRICH BLUME

Translated by
STANLEY GODMAN

DA CAPO PRESS · NEW YORK · 1978

Library of Congress Cataloging in Publication Data

Blume, Friedrich, 1893-
  Two centuries of Bach, an account of changing taste.

  (Da Capo Press music reprint series)
  Reprint of the 1950 ed. published by Oxford
University Press, London.
  Translation of Johann Sebastian Bach im Wandel der
Geschichte.
  1. Bach, Johann Sebastian, 1685-1750. I. Title.
[ML410.B1B6512 1978]   780'.92'4   77-27291
ISBN 0-306-77567-0

Published by Da Capo Press, Inc.
A Subsidiary of Plenum Publishing Corporation
227 West 17th Street, New York, N.Y. 10011

10-09-78

Two Centuries
of Bach

Two Centuries of Bach

of Bach

AN ACCOUNT OF CHANGING TASTE

By

FRIEDRICH BLUME

D.PH., PROFESSOR OF MUSICOLOGY IN
THE UNIVERSITY OF KIEL

Translated by
STANLEY GODMAN

GEOFFREY CUMBERLEGE
OXFORD UNIVERSITY PRESS
LONDON   NEW YORK   TORONTO
1950

Oxford University Press, Amen House, London E.C.4

GLASGOW NEW YORK TORONTO MELBOURNE WELLINGTON
BOMBAY CALCUTTA MADRAS CAPE TOWN

Geoffrey Cumberlege, Publisher to the University

This book was originally published in 1947
*by Bärenreiter-Verlag, Kassel, under the
title of* Johann Sebastian Bach im Wandel
der Geschichte

PRINTED IN GREAT BRITAIN

THE POSTHUMOUS FAME AND INFLUENCE OF GREAT creative personalities depends on a complex of forces, the interaction of which can sometimes be seen in the simple form of two parallel and complementary forces. More often, however, the influence of a great creative mind widens out into a much more complicated and involved network. The first of the active forces working after a great artist's own lifetime, what we might call the warp in the texture of his influence, is the personality and achievement of the artist himself. His character, his nature, his life with all its mystery of fate and chance, the immediate attractiveness or the strangeness of his work as well as the purely human qualities of the man, his traditionalism or individualism, his acceptance or rejection of contemporary society—all these factors affect his subsequent influence, including that on his own immediate contemporaries.

The second active force in this complex of influences on which an artist's posthumous fame depends, the first thread in the woof, is the attitude adopted by those who come under his immediate influence, his contemporaries and sympathizers. Their goodwill, their interest, their recognition or condemnation of his work, their understanding or lack of understanding, their favour and their verdict, their acceptance or rejection of the great genius in their midst, all these factors must be sufficiently positive and constructive for the great man's influence to be transmitted directly, without any obstacle, to later generations. There have been great artists enough in history who have made their way with their own contemporaries and descendants by no deliberate effort on their part, purely and simply by the natural exercise of their own gifts and powers, as for instance (to confine ourselves to examples from musical history, although it would probably be as easy to quote from the history of literature or the plastic arts): Palestrina, Heinrich Schütz, Handel, and Beethoven. Opposition, if it raised its head at all, was nipped in the bud. The customary and traditional elements in the work and personality of such artists were familiar and agreeable to all; the new elements which they proclaimed in their works, even if they seemed utterly revolutionary to their contemporaries, made their way with such eruptive force that the barriers of misunderstanding or malevolence, of personal jealousy and malice, were simply hurled on one side. Their influence was so convincing and overwhelming that even later generations have never or scarcely ever seriously disputed their pre-eminence.

6

Their fame, even though it may have faded for a time, has never suffered any serious eclipse. Other artists, on the other hand, have had to struggle against the violent opposition of their contemporaries, the conflict of opinion has flared up around them in their own lifetime and hardly ever settled down at all. All the same they found ways and means of achieving a hard-won victory, by fighting with all the resources of creative work and teaching, with all the powers of the written and spoken word, and even by using as a last resort the influence of advertisement, propaganda, and intrigue. By such means they made their posthumous fame and influence secure. Such men were Schumann and Liszt, Gluck and Berlioz, Monteverdi and Richard Wagner. Novel and strange forces erupted from these artists with such elemental and terrifying force, the links with the past seemed to be so completely broken in their works, and the revolutionary element so deliberate, that they inevitably struck a wall of ignorance and misunderstanding, of conservative scorn and condemnation. Only by relentless attack and embittered self-defence were they able to overcome this opposition. When the opposition had been finally overcome, however, the contemporary world bowed in submission to their greatness and transmitted their fame to later generations. Different again was the pattern of posthumous fame in the case of a third group of artists, who, either because of

7

other-worldly asceticism or ecstatic absorption in their own work and mission, or simply because of unfavourable external circumstances, ignored their own contemporaries or were unable to convince them, because they lacked the fighting instinct, were too sensitive or retiring to overwhelm them by using the finer or the coarser methods of persuasion, and finally gave up the struggle. The surprising thing is that their greatness was soon proclaimed by a younger generation of enthusiasts. Schubert and Chopin, Mozart and Bruckner were examples of this type of genius. These are the men of whom it is frequently stated that they were in advance of their own time—a false conception of history, for no one can be in advance of his own time. Is it not that their own contemporaries lagged behind them in a state of artistic stagnation? That is the reason why this third group appears predominantly at the time of the early Romantic movement when, as a result of the early stages of industrialism, the dull-witted masses were out of touch with intellectual and cultural activities and could not keep step with the impetuous advances which were being made in the arts.

We come now to the third active force which has a decisive effect on the posthumous life and influence of great men of genius, what we may call the second thread in the woof, namely, the verdict of the next generation. The next, not the later generations. These later generations constantly reshape the image of the great man as it has been passed on to them, they add their own variations to the form and shape of his genius but they no longer dispute the actual greatness of the man or only very rarely. The generation which immediately follows the lifetime of a great genius, however, delivers its own judgement on him, and it is a misfortune if later generations accept this verdict without having first considered it very carefully. If they do we then get those tragic cases in which the great man, whether he was recognized by his contemporaries or not, falls into oblivion along with the rest of his own generation, simply because his younger contemporaries no longer take any notice of him and no longer understand him. It is then left to much later generations to rediscover the greatness of the man and his work. It is easy to illustrate this process by recalling the names of a fourth group of artists whose fate it has been, first to be tragically forgotten, and then to rise again in glory after many generations. Masters of the highest standing like Lasso, Buxtehude, Lechner, and many others were forgotten, only to come to light again centuries after their death: Rameau in France, Telemann in Germany, worshipped by their own contemporaries, died with their own generation and fell into complete oblivion until musicologists of the last few decades raised them up again to their rightful status in the history of music.

Even Haydn, the recognized and undisputed leader of the whole musical world in Europe at the turn of the eighteenth century, succumbed to the lack of understanding shown by the following generation, and his work was forgotten owing to their lack of judgement. It was a hundred years before historical research brought it to light again.

It is clear that the network of influences emanating from the work of a great creative artist is complicated enough already. Yet to the judgement of the following generation we have now to add, as a further thread in the woof, the verdict of that generation's grandchildren and great-grandchildren as it varies through the changes of history, changes which are clearly reflected in the varying conceptions of greatness held by each succeeding generation. Two facts contribute to the formation of the posthumous 'image' of a great genius. The first is the fact that the changing generations and historical epochs constantly reshape the 'image' in the light of their own needs and problems. The 'image' itself is therefore involved in a process of flux and change. The second is the fact, the more remarkable fact, that despite all the varying attitudes of the changing generations, once the greatness of a man has been acknowledged it is never in serious danger, even though the 'image' which each succeeding generation creates for itself is subject to the strongest possible variations. In other words, a certain essence of greatness remains unimpaired through all the processes of change.

History cannot be understood without taking into account this polarity of permanence and change, of undeviating continuity and undulating rhythm. Does not what we call 'historical greatness' consist precisely in the fact that it is variable enough to enable it to be transmitted to many different generations and to reveal previously neglected aspects of greatness as time goes on, and in the fact that it is also permanent and stable enough to preserve its innermost essence unchanged and unquestioned through the centuries, unaffected by the varying ideas which each generation creates for itself?

Like all generalizations this 'law' of historical greatness as we may call it is only partly applicable to the actual facts of each individual case. The posthumous life of Bach is evidence of its partial validity as well as of its partial inapplicability. The changes undergone by Bach in the course of time since his death reveal just as much the characteristics of his own nature as the characteristic ideologies of the later generations of which the changing 'images' of his greatness are the reflection.

Sebastian Bach was about fifty years old when the literary controversy about him arose which an observant contemporary would have recognized as the storm signal of imminent crises and revolutions in the

world of music. The followings words of J. Adolf
Scheibe written in 1737 in section six of his paper
Critischer Musicus, without actually naming either
himself or the object of his attack, though both were
obvious to the initiated, were intended as a challenge
but were interpreted as a manifesto.

This great man [he wrote] would be the admiration of whole
nations if he had more amenity, if he did not take away the
natural elements in his pieces by giving them a turgid and
confused style, and if he did not darken their beauty by an
excess of art. . . . Every ornament, every little grace, and everything that one thinks of as belonging to the method of playing,
he expresses completely in notes; and this not only takes away
from his pieces the beauty of harmony but completely covers
the melody throughout. In short, he is in music what Mr. von
Lohenstein was in poetry. Turgidity has led them both from
the natural to the artificial, and from the lofty to the sombre;
and in both one admires the onerous labour and uncommon
effort—which, however, are vainly employed, since they conflict with Reason.

This invective can hardly have surprised Bach himself
very much. He knew perfectly well how he stood with
his immediate contemporaries and the younger generation. What gave the pamphlet its particularly strik-
ing note, however, was the fact that Scheibe was not
a mere nonentity but the acknowledged spokesman
of the younger generation of musicians and that his
paper was the leading musical journal, highly valued
by Gottsched, quoted by Lessing, and with which men

like Marpurg in Berlin and Mattheson in Hamburg were at any rate closely associated.

Scheibe was attempting nothing less than the creation of a completely new theoretical foundation for music. In his system of aesthetics the traditional unity of divine law, cosmic number-symbolism, and the combined crafts of music and mathematics on which European music had been based for a thousand years was replaced by the rule of reason and feeling. Transcendence was replaced by immanence, God-centred by man-centred music. In Scheibe's criticism we have the whole vocabulary of the new philosophy of music expressed in slogans: 'reason' striving against the 'labour' of the intellect, 'beauty' against 'art', 'sublimity' against 'obscurity', 'confusion' against 'agreeableness'. The musician with purely 'natural' feeling who only wants the simple beauty of melody feels himself infinitely superior to the tangled figures and complicated counterpoint, the old lumber of fugues and canons from 'grandfather's old attic'. Classical sobriety rises up against the wealth of formal subtleties of the Baroque, the simple beat of the human heart against the world of symbols which is now regarded as nothing more than the lumber of the outmoded formulae of coldly calculating intellects. In another place Scheibe describes the great period of Flemish polyphony at the end of the Middle Ages, to which Bach gave a real 'resurrection of the dead' in his later works, as the lowest point ever reached in the history of music. He declares that melody went under in a morass of simultaneous lines and that it is now the task of musicians to revive 'the sweet pleasantness of melody'. With Hasse and Graun 'a new period of music' begins, according to Scheibe (an observation which reveals his amazingly clear historical insight). The old gods have fallen. A new day calls to fresh fields and pastures new. Bach's work is all in vain: his aims are fundamentally wrong. 'The composer who does not think naturally may arouse a certain admiration by his hard work, but he will not move his audience, will not leave behind with them an impression and an emotion.' That is as contrary to Bach's philosophy as possible. He was not concerned with the impression made by his music, he regarded his art as a form of service, whereas the new music was wholly intent on moving the human heart. Two worlds were breaking apart from each other and it was still a long way yet to Goethe's 'Nature and Art seem to be fleeing from each other and in no time they have found their way back to each other again'. In Scheibe's words the younger generation was passing judgement on Bach. The 'Jesu juva' and 'Soli deo gloria' which Bach was in the habit of putting at the end of his works no longer meant anything at all to them: first, because they had broken away from religion and the Church, secondly because these formulae expressed an attitude to music diametrically opposed to their own. Not the metaphysical world of divine order, but man with his reason and his heart were now to be the standard of musical value. In these writings of Scheibe the foundations were laid on which the whole structure of modern music is based, from the age of sentimental 'galanterie' to the age of the Vienna classics, from the Romantic movement in all its various stages right up to the music of our own time. Beginning with the generation of Bach's sons the whole of the younger generation of musicians had inevitably to turn away from Bach if they were to be honest with themselves. Scheibe saw that perfectly correctly from the point of view of the younger men. It is obvious that their point of view was one-sided, but it is the prerogative of youth to be one-sided; and when Magister Birnbaum, who set himself up as Bach's defender against the attacks of Scheibe, attempted to patch up and explain away the conflict between the two worlds it was Birnbaum who was in the wrong. There was nothing there to patch up or bridge over. It was the most violent breach that had ever split the history of European culture in two.

Scheibe was by no means the only one thinking along these lines. He was speaking in the name of all his immediate contemporaries; Bach's own sons failed to understand their father. The ugly phrase about 'the old wig' which is attributed to the youngest of his sons, J. Christian, the renegade, the Catholic, and the leading spirit in the world of 'sentimental' music, is difficult to verify and may be based on gossip. But even his second-eldest son, Philipp Emanuel, a man of judgement and distinction, says about his father in a letter written in 1775: 'Altogether he did not have the most brilliant good fortune because he did not do the one thing that is really essential, namely, roam about the world.' This son who knew his father very intimately and left us many trustworthy accounts of his life and work was already so far removed from a true understanding of him that he did not appreciate the significance of his father's deep-rooted love of his native soil which is one of the most vital points in his character. Philipp Emanuel's contemporary fame exceeded that of his father. With their dashing compositions and their virtuosity as pianists he and his eldest brother Wilhelm Friedemann were the exact opposite of their father. When Philipp Emanuel says:

A player cannot move others unless he is moved himself . . . that this cannot come off properly without corresponding gestures, only he will deny who is constrained by his lack of sensitivity to sit in front of the instrument like a carved image,

he is obviously hitting at his father, whose impersonal and measured style of playing was an expression of the power of mind over feeling, in fact of the complete incompatibility of his whole musical outlook with any kind of sentiment. Even Quantz thought the same as Bach's sons about the older generation. 'Bach's sons were children of their age and never understood their father', wrote the music historian Robert Eitner in 1885. But even such a highly cultivated man as J. A. Hiller, Bach's third successor as Cantor of St. Thomas's, Leipzig, had only a few very superficial remarks to make about the master of organ and fugue in his autobiography (1784). In another place he coolly admits that Bach's Church compositions did honour to his 'profound mind' and needed to be properly appreciated by 'their own lovers'. That Hiller was not one of them we are assured by Zelter who tells us that he 'tried to fill the lads of the St. Thomas choir with loathing for the crudities of Bach'. And that was a man who was supposed to be the official custodian of Bach's Cantatas and Passions. The Prussian Court Kapellmeister Reichardt even went so far as to say in 1782:

If Bach had had the high sense of truth and the deep feeling for expression that inspired Handel, he would have become a far greater man than Handel. As it is, however, he is merely more highly skilled technically and more hard-working.

The break with the younger generation was unavoidable. With his sturdy self-confidence Bach felt himself to be the final representative of an age-old philosophy of music in the midst of a rapidly changing world. For him there was nothing irregular or accidental in music, nothing that did not subserve a higher purpose and a regulated order, nothing, moreover, that merely flattered the senses, moved sentimental souls to tears, or was merely the outpouring of the wretched little human heart. Bach was the centre into which everything flowed that had been thought, done, known, and willed in a thousand years of music before him. Everything that had been added to this inheritance by his own age flowed into him too. He was fully aware of his culminating and retrospective position in musical history. He also knew that the whole world-order of which he was the ultimate consummation had come to an end with him. With such knowledge in his mind he trod the path which led in the last twenty years of his life to the completion of his historical mission, deliberately renouncing the laurels which he might easily have gathered by the wayside. Conscious of his mission he purposely turned his back on all the aims and ideals of the new world of music and in these twenty years created the works in which he gave a final monumental expression to the inheritance of a thousand years, the last Church Cantatas, the Organ Chorale Preludes, the Variations on 'Vom Himmel hoch', the *Goldberg Variations*, the *Musical Offering*, and the *Art of Fugue*. He was not a resigned and disillusioned man. He stood in the very midst of active life. He did not despise his own age, in fact he was the friend of Telemann, Hasse, Graun, Zelenka, Benda, and others and performed their works. But he saw quite clearly that all the old valid foundations of music and

18

of the world-order in general were about to be turned completely upside down, and he saw all the more clearly the divine command, the 'office' in the Lutheran sense of the word, and the historical mission committed to his charge. Out of the fullness of life he turned backwards therefore and erected the final memorials to a dying millennium of music in the seclusion of his composing room in St. Thomas's School in Leipzig. If the younger generation broke the one essential thread in the woof of his posthumous fame, he himself broke the warp in the web, fully conscious that posterity could wreathe no garlands in honour of the kind of work which he had accomplished in the Leipzig years.

It was not only the younger generation which sat in judgement on Bach. The verdict of his own contemporaries and of his own society was also against Bach the composer. The fame which he acquired amongst his contemporaries was as an organist and harpsichordist, as a dreaded technical expert and adviser on the organ, as an uncanny master of the art of counterpoint, as a teacher, but not as the composer of the Cantatas and Passions, of the *Mass in B minor*, and of the Organ Chorale Preludes, nor even as the composer of the concertos, sonatas, and suites. The period of his life on which such fame as he acquired was based was from 1708 to 1716 when he was Kammerorganist in Weimar, and, though only to a lesser degree, the Cöthen period from 1717 to 1722 when he was Hofkapellmeister; in other words, the period of his youth and the early years of his life as a professional musician. In the last twenty-seven years of his life which he spent in Leipzig, a city with an important university, with the leading Lutheran clergy, with annual trade fairs and a cultivated middle class with a wide outlook, a city of students and artists, in all these years not a single word of appreciation, of praise, or even of mere acknowledgement of Bach the composer is heard. Not one word about the Passions or Cantatas, not one word about the four published sections of the *Clavierübung*, or about the numerous festival compositions and serenades, about the motets or the organ works, not to mention the *Musical Offering* or the *Art of Fugue*. Leipzig and the whole of Germany completely ignored the greatest composer of the age. The silence could not have been any deeper if his compositions had never existed at all. When the position of Cantor of St. Thomas's became vacant again after Kuhnau's death, long negotiations were conducted with Telemann and Graupner, both of whom received the most generous offers. Bach, although he was available and fresh from his post as Hofkapellmeister in Cöthen, was only considered at the very last and then with a regretful sigh, 'As the best are not available, I suppose we must take one of the second-rate men.' This remark made by Dr. Platz, the mayor of Leipzig, expressed the general feeling of the City Council. Gottsched, who worked side by side with Bach in Leipzig for twenty-seven years and wrote innumerable Cantata libretti, did not write a single one for Bach (the fact that Bach composed the Funeral Ode to the Electress Christiane Eberhardine was due to chance). Gottsched was an enthusiastic admirer of Scheibe, Marpurg, and Hasse and was able to write *In Praise of Germania*:

> Did not Sturm think out the order of German columns?
> Are not Telemann and Handel well known?
> Even Zeuxis himself will give the wreath of victory to
> Holbein's art and Cranach's magic hand.

Not a word for, not even a word about, Bach. When the sixty-four-year-old master lay seriously ill, a year before his death, his ultimate successor Gottlob Harrer was summoned in June 1749 to undergo the public examination for the appointment as Cantor of St. Thomas's 'in case the Kapellmeister and Cantor Herr Sebastian Bach should die'—a cold douche for the old man which was contrary to all good manners and all tradition. When, to the perceptible relief of the whole of Leipzig, Bach finally closed his eyes on 28 July 1750, Dr. Stieglitz, the mayor, expressed the views of the public in the following plain words: 'The school needs a cantor, not a Kapellmeister, despite the fact that he must understand music [i.e. composition].' As early as the early 1730's there had been increasing signs of discord: disputes with and around Bach grew in intensity, were made the most of and exaggerated, and never brought to a satisfactory conclusion. No doubt they were caused partly by Bach's own quarrelsome nature, by his stubborn insistence on his rights, but the deeper reasons are to be sought in those revolutionary changes in the world of music which like a thunder-cloud were heralding the approach of a new age. Scheibe was in fact quite right: 'a new period' was dawning but not only in the world of music. It was not merely the whole attitude to the arts that was changing: the whole world of class and privilege, of Lutheran orthodoxy and Christian theocracy, the world of what Valentin Loescher had called 'good order', was collapsing, undermined by the progress of the Enlightenment. It was a foregone conclusion on which side Sebastian Bach would inevitably take his stand. But by their very acceptance of his position as an obvious matter of course, his own society and his own fellows had pronounced judgement on him: he belonged, they said, to a world that was falling into ruins. Bach stood in full view of the public eye. For nearly thirty years he worked among his fellow citizens, conducting Passions and Cantatas in the two main churches, directing splendid festival concerts in the market square, organizing chamber-music concerts by his undergraduate Collegium Musicum in Zimmermann's coffee-house or in the coffee-gardens outside the city

walls, composing and improvising. In spite of all this
public work he was half-forgotten in his own lifetime,
and regarded as an intractable oddity, a sarcastic old
fogey. Telemann was paying him a quite exceptional
compliment when he said of him in the verse obituary
which he wrote in a spirit of the truest friendship:

> Departed Bach! Long since thy splendid organ playing
> Alone brought thee the noble cognomen 'the Great',
> And what thy pen had writ, the highest art displaying,
> Did some with joy and some with envy contemplate.
> Then sleep! The candle of thy fame ne'er low will burn,
> The pupils thou hast trained and those they train in turn
> Prepare thy future crown of glory brightly glowing.
> Thy children's hands adorn it with its jewels bright,
> But what shall cause thy true worth to be judged aright
> Berlin to us now in a worthy son is showing.[1]

That is the point: the organ virtuoso, the master of the
arts of counterpoint, the teacher, but, between the
lines, unsaid but quite plain to those with ears to hear,
Telemann is saying that in his opinion Philipp Emanuel
is a much more important figure than his father.
Together with Bach and Handel, Telemann forms
the great musical triad of the age. If even he who was
Bach's close friend for a whole lifetime thought like
that, what could be expected of lesser spirits? Handel,
whom Bach positively courted, never once took the

---

[1] Reprinted from *The Bach Reader* by David and Mendel, by permission of Messrs. J. M. Dent & Sons Ltd., Letchworth, and of Messrs.
W. W. Norton, New York.

slightest notice of the little German Cantor and Kapellmeister. The whole age had not the slightest inkling
of Bach's greatness. It would be foolish to touch up
this picture of heart-rending solitude and cruel lack of
understanding among his own immediate fellows, as
the excellent Bach scholar, Arnold Schering, is inclined to do in the idyllic portrayal of Bach given in
his last comprehensive work on *The Musical History of
Leipzig in the Age of Bach and Hiller* (1941).[1] His conception of Bach is distorted and liable to confuse and
upset our conception of the historical facts.

Popular expositions of Bach are in the habit of
spreading the idea that Bach's personality and works
were forgotten after his death and not discovered again
until sometime in the nineteenth century. That view
of the matter is not entirely supported by historical
research. For the most part there was in fact nothing
of Bach's work to be forgotten because it had never
been really known; but, on the other hand, his achieve-
ments were never completely forgotten. It is easy to
appreciate why the musicians of the *galant* and sentimental age from Graun to Reichardt, from Bach's own
sons to the Haydn of the middle period, as well as
the gradually developing Vienna classics, could have
nothing to do with him and ignored him, preoccupied
as they were with their own progress and achieve-
ments. It is true, of course, that during his time in

[1] *Musikgeschichte Leipzigs im Zeitalter Bachs und Hillers.*

Halle, Friedemann Bach still performed isolated cantatas by his father, though in greatly revised arrangements and only as a stopgap; on the other hand, Zelter
says that he never heard Friedemann, whom he calls
'the most perfect organist', 'play a note of his father's
music, much as everyone wanted him to'. When in
the years 1771–4 he fell on evil days Friedemann had
to sell the manuscripts inherited from his father.
Philipp Emanuel grew out of the family tradition so
quickly that he had to admit to Charles Burney in
1773 that he had become completely estranged from
the organ. In his twenty-three years as the leading
musician in Hamburg it never occurred to him to
perform a single one of his father's works. For a
Matthew Passion in 1769 he unscrupulously plundered
his father's work and some of his cantatas and allowed
the pastiche to go out under his own name. When we
remember that, on the other hand, Philipp Emanuel
was one of the first Germans to revive or rather to
naturalize Handel by performing *Messiah* in 1775
and 1777 in Hamburg, a work which up to that time
had so far received only one hearing there under Dr.
Arne, the change of outlook becomes quite clear.
Philipp Emanuel did at least faithfully preserve his
father's manuscripts and they later reached the Prussian
State Library in Berlin by way of the book-collector
Georg Pölchau. There is not the slightest evidence,
however, that Bach's sons ever took even the most

elementary practical interest in his compositions. If even his two eldest sons completely failed to take any interest in them, the lack of interest shown by his younger sons, such as Christoph Friedrich and Johann Christian, the converted apostate, who spent his life in England, is hardly surprising. They were all important figures in their time, leaders of the younger generation, but, as Eitner says, completely the 'children of their age'. Their only claim to be considered in the history of Bach's posthumous fame is in so far as they preserved his works in manuscript and passed on a fairly reliable memory of his personality.

In the Thomas School, however, a modest rivulet of the Bach tradition trickled on. During the Cantorship of Doles (1756–89) Bach Cantatas were still very occasionally performed. When, on the other hand, Neefe, who was later to become Beethoven's teacher, reported to his friend Schubart in Ulm in 1776 that Doles intended to perform a Bach Passion, it is, to say the least, doubtful whether he meant Sebastian Bach at all.

Simply because they were exceptionally difficult and made good show-pieces for the St. Thomas choir, Bach's Motets, above all *Singet dem Herrn*, kept their place in the repertory for a time, contrary though they were to the general taste of the age. In this connexion we have the well-known anecdote about Mozart hearing this Motet sung under Doles when he was passing through Leipzig in 1789 and raging with enthusiasm over it. One of the Thomas choristers at the time was Friedrich Rochlitz, who later corresponded with Goethe on musical subjects and became an accomplished writer on music. Nearly forty years later he gave an account of the incident from memory.

Mozart [he wrote] knew Bach more by hearsay than by his works, at least his motets, which had never been printed, were completely unknown to him. Hardly had the choir sung a few measures when Mozart sat up startled, a few measures more and he called out, 'What is this?' And now his whole soul seemed to be in his ears. When the singing was finished he cried out, full of joy, 'Now there is something one can learn from.' He was told that this school in which Sebastian Bach had been Cantor possessed the complete collection of his motets and preserved them as a sort of sacred relic. 'That's the spirit, that's fine!' he cried. 'Let's see them!'—There was, however, no score of these songs, so he had the parts given to him, and then for the silent observer it was a joy to see how eagerly Mozart sat himself down, with the parts all around him, in both hands, on his knees and on the chairs next to him; and forgetting everything else, he did not get up again until he had looked through everything of Sebastian Bach's that was there. He asked for a copy and valued it very highly.

For Mozart, however, Bach had already become more than a name by this time. The Director of the Court Library in Vienna, Baron van Swieten, had joined a circle of Bach enthusiasts, including Marpurg, Kirnberger, and others, when he was a diplomat in Berlin. In his house in Vienna the 'learned' music was

eagerly studied; in other words, the arts of counterpoint provided the members of his circle with high-
class entertainment. Perhaps through the agency
of Kirnberger, himself a former pupil of Bach, van
Swieten possessed a number of the master's works.
In 1782 Mozart reported that he went 'every Sunday
at noon to Baron van Swieten's house where nothing
is played but Handel and Bach'. Mozart made copies
of Bach fugues for himself, studied them eagerly, and
arranged them for strings. Even Constanze was full of
enthusiasm for them. Mozart also made the acquain-
tance of the organ trios and pieces from the *Art of
Fugue*. After his death the second part of the *Clavierübung*, the Italian Concerto, and the Partita in B minor
were found amongst his scores. It is clear from this
that his knowledge of Bach was confined, as with the
Motets, to the contrapuntal side of his work. For
Mozart, as for the others, it was Bach the master of
fugue who aroused his astonishment and appealed to
his understanding. How profoundly Mozart's assimi-
lation of Bach influenced his work and therefore made
musical history! From the String Quartet in G major
and the Serenade for wind instruments in C minor (both
written in 1782!) to the *Mass in C minor*, from the
'Jupiter' Symphony to *The Magic Flute* an increasingly
powerful influence makes itself felt in his work. Even
before the revival of the historical Bach, his work was
beginning to fertilize the music of the new age.

Bach's influence on Haydn follows similar lines but is not so easy to define. Haydn was still far more at home in the van Swieten circle where he, too, became acquainted with the works of Bach and Handel. In fact, he possessed not only Nägeli's first edition of the 'Forty Eight' (1801) but also the Motets, and, most unusual for his time, a copy of the *Mass in B minor*. Obviously at the suggestion of van Swieten, the Vienna music publisher Traeg supplied copies of Bach's works. In addition to arranging the libretti for *The Creation* and *The Seasons* van Swieten also provided Haydn with models for the music by introducing him to Bach and Handel. The two most popular German Oratorios are, like the six great Masses of Haydn's closing years, inconceivable without the influence of Bach. Haydn travelled a strange route: the man from Lower Austria who admitted that he had learnt from only one man during his apprenticeship in Vienna, namely, from Bach's son Philipp Emanuel, who worked in Hamburg and whom Haydn never met, became, when he was fifty years old, the spiritual disciple of Sebastian Bach himself. In Haydn's work the style of Viennese classicism is fused with the legacy of the 'forgotten' Bach, though Haydn himself still thinks of Bach simply as the 'patriarch of harmony' and the master of counterpoint.

Without the influence of Bach, Beethoven's later works are even less conceivable than those of Haydn and Mozart. As a twelve-year-old boy Beethoven was introduced to the 'Forty Eight' by Christian Gottlob Neefe, who as a student in Leipzig had come into touch with the Doles circle, and as early as 1783 he was already playing many of the pieces 'quite perfectly'. At the social evenings which he attended at Baron van Swieten's house, he was always kept back very late to play 'still more of Sebastian Bach's fugues as an evening benediction'. He remained faithful to the 'Forty Eight' throughout his life and he studied the *Chromatic Fantasia* and the *Art of Fugue* in detail. He must also have known the *Mass in B minor* since his own *Missa Solemnis* is inconceivable without its influence. He possessed the 'Forty Eight', the fifteen Symphonies and Inventions, and three books of 'Exercises' (probably the *Clavierübung*), as we learn from Anton Schindler. In addition to all this interest in Bach he also took an active part in the early preparations towards a revival of Bach's works. In his letters he repeatedly pressed the firm of Breitkopf and Härtel to print Bach's works—until about 1800 there was, in fact, almost nothing of the whole of Bach's output in print—and he subscribed in advance for anything that was likely to appear. He greeted the announcement of a complete edition by Hoffmeister and Kühnel in 1806 with intense enthusiasm. (It was the edition planned by Forkel.) When Rochlitz appealed for funds to support Bach's only surviving daughter who was in dire need, Beethoven was one of the first to send a contribution. In his later works, the piano sonatas in A flat major and B flat major, the *Missa Solemnis*, the last string quartets, and other works besides, he was deeply indebted to Bach. If any additional proof is required, then the sketch-book in which he entered the plan for an overture on B A C H while he was working on the Ninth Symphony in 1822 provides it.

Even though these were all only narrow rivulets through which Bach's compositions trickled on, they gained immense significance by penetrating so deeply into the works of the Vienna masters, which came to be regarded by the whole world as classical and authoritative. Little as Bach had been able to secure recognition for his work in his own lifetime, as a substantial element in the musical blood of the Vienna masters it quickly flowed into the circulation of world music. Other rivulets were trickling along besides, however, almost subterranean, hardly visible, and not flowing directly into the outward events of the time. But they are no less important, for through them the greatest part of Bach's work was first transmitted to posterity, and through them at least an outline of his life and personality was passed on. Haydn, Mozart, and Beethoven cannot have had any more than the vaguest idea of Bach's personality; of his real nature and character, of the purpose and intentions of his music they definitely had not the slightest idea. It is obvious, of course, that the whole world in this age of Enlightenment, which had no sense of history in any case, had not the slightest idea of Bach's historical significance. Those, however, who did hand on, quietly and faithfully, some conception of his personality and great parts of his work, were, as Telemann had quite correctly foreseen, 'the pupils thou hast trained and those they train in turn', men like H. Nicolaus Gerber, the father of the famous lexicographer, Tobias and his son Ludwig Krebs ('the best crayfish [Krebs] in my brook [Bach]'); J. Friedrich Agricola, who with Philipp Emanuel wrote the *Necrology* in memory of Bach; J. Friedrich Doles, his second successor as Cantor of St. Thomas's; Gottfried August Homilius, later Cantor of the School of the Holy Cross in Dresden; J. Philipp Kirnberger, music master to Princess Amalie of Prussia, who was the fiercest character among the group who carried on the Bach tradition in Berlin and who recorded memories of Bach's own teaching in his treatise *On the Art of Pure Setting* (1774–9);[1] J. Gottfried Goldberg, to whom the Variations were dedicated; J. Christoph Altnikol, who became Bach's son-in-law in 1749 and took down his last compositions; and finally J. Christoph Kittel, who was only eighteen when Bach died and who carried the Bach tradition right on into the nineteenth cen-

[1] *Die Kunst des reinen Satzes.*

tury. A solid group of Bach disciples was centred round these pupils of the master in Berlin, the most devoted members of which were Frederick the Great's sister Amalie, Kirnberger, Philipp Emanuel, and later on, as guest-members, Friedemann Bach, Marpurg, and several others. In this circle Bach's works were passed from hand to hand, copied out again and again, and these copies reached the hands of all the north and central German organists of the time. Most of the original sources for the 'Forty Eight', the Fantasias, the organ Chorale Preludes, the many preludes and fugues for organ, the instrumental concertos, the keyboard suites, &c., which have come down to the present day were derived originally from this circle of devoted enthusiasts. Bach's organ and keyboard works, his organ technique and at least some idea of his personality and mind were passed on from them to later generations. In 1773 Charles Burney was able to report:

All organists now living in Germany have modelled themselves on his school, just as most of the pianists have modelled themselves on his son, the excellent Philipp Emanuel Bach.

From the narrow channels through which the fame of Bach was transmitted in Leipzig, Vienna, and Berlin, the publishers also received a slight impulse. Like Traeg in Vienna, Breitkopf and Härtel in Leipzig, Westphal, Rellstab, and others in Berlin sold manuscript copies of Bach's works. The periphery of the

Berlin circle reached as far as Riga and Königsberg in the north-east, through Neefe it reached as far as Bonn in the west, and through van Swieten as far as Vienna in the south. But it was an esoteric circle. The initiated had no desire to make converts outside their own circle, regarded themselves as prophets, stubbornly shut themselves off from the music of the new age and inclined (Kirnberger in particular) to aggressive outbursts of invective. They served the cause of Bach by preserving his works intact amongst themselves, not by any direct impact on the outside world. This Bach cult is illuminated by the very similar anecdotes which are told about Kittel and Kirnberger:

A very well executed oil painting of J. Sebastian Bach which he had hung over his piano served as a curious kind of reward or punishment for his pupils. If the pupil showed himself worthy, by his industry, of this father of harmony, the curtain which covered it was raised. For the unworthy, on the other hand, Bach's countenance remained covered.

From the hands of these pupils and priests of Bach the legacy passed to the younger disciples, to Hering, Kellner, Fischhof, Forkel, Pölchau, and many others, and from them it was taken over, right up to the last war, by the German public libraries.

There is no need to expatiate here on the immense importance of this channel of the Bach tradition for the later Bach revival. No less a writer than E. T. A. Hoffmann is evidence of the distinguished influence on artistic and creative life exerted by these Bach enthusiasts, for indirectly he owed his knowledge of and enthusiasm for Bach to the Bach circle in Berlin. His teacher Podbielski in Königsberg was a descendant of one of Bach's pupils. Hoffmann's Bach cult is also esoteric. Kapellmeister Kreisler washes himself clean in Bach's music when, after he has had to sit through a session of shallow tea-party gossip, he plays the *Goldberg Variations* to his flabbergasted audience who were expecting the latest flashy drawing-room variations. The *Kreisleriana, Kater Murr,* and many other books are evidence of Hoffmann's enthusiasm for Bach, and in them are also the first signs of a new romanticizing attitude to Bach. For Hoffmann music is already a 'religious cult' in itself—and that really prevented him from penetrating to Bach's innermost spirit.

The rivulets through which a limited and modest Bach tradition flowed after his death were very narrow. The tradition which they passed on was confined almost entirely to parts of the organ and keyboard works. The memory of the man himself was dim. The idea that was current at the time was no different from the one held in the main by his own contemporaries of the Leipzig years, who thought of him as a musician of uncanny ability and infallible technical skill, as an astonishing organ virtuoso and a brilliant harpsichordist, as a stern teacher and a profound contrapuntist. The human conception of the man had long since been lost to view, and most of his contemporaries would not have retained any more accurate memory of him than did that honest Leipzig linen-draper who saw the oil-painting of Bach hanging in Kirnberger's room and cried out:

Why, good Lord, you've actually got our Cantor Bach hanging there; we have him too in Leipzig at the Thomas School. They say he was a rough fellow: didn't the conceited fool even go and have himself painted in a smart velvet coat?

Whereupon the infuriated Kirnberger threw him down the staircase. No one really penetrated to the heart of Bach's work and personality and the substance of his art remained shrouded in impenetrable darkness.

Before Bach could be seen in a different light a completely new way of thinking was required. A new sense of history was needed before a new phase in the history of the Bach tradition could begin. It came at last during the period of the Napoleonic Wars and it came from four directions. In the first place, it was the dawn of a passionate love for the old German traditions, of a new interest in history and of a new discipline of historical study, of an insatiable urge to rediscover the sources of history: in a word, it was the spirit which created the 'Monumenta Germaniae' which introduced a new phase in the development of the Bach problem. In the second place, it was the surge of a new attitude to the world taking hold of men's hearts, releasing them from the bonds of rationalism and aspiring to experience the world emotionally, placing art above man (as Wackenroder put it) and seeing in music (as E. T. A. Hoffmann put it) a mysterious realm of spirits, a world of aesthetic self-sufficiency beyond reality. With flamboyant exuberance the questionable and dangerous quality of 'absolute' existence was attributed to every kind of music and Bach himself was avowed the king of such a supernatural realm of spirits. In the third place, the powerful rise of national consciousness in the period of the Napoleonic Wars opened the eyes of the Germans to the national and popular content and values of music and taught them to see in Bach the prototype of the German spirit in music. In the fourth place, soon after 1800 a new wave of religious fervour began to spread through Protestant Germany, a new kind of religious emotion appeared in the wake of neo-pietism or the revival movement, as it is sometimes called. It permeated the whole attitude to life of the new age and led to the discovery of Bach the church musician. If a new conception of Bach was to be achieved anywhere, all these four streams had to meet.

In the person of Johann Nikolaus Forkel, the director of music in the University of Göttingen, the first approach to the historical study of music was made. He followed the example set by the Göttingen school of universal history and tried to understand musical history as a part of the general history of culture. In his unfinished *History of Music* (1788, 1801) he undertook to do for music what other members of the Göttingen school, Fiorillo and Bouterweg, had done for the plastic arts and literature respectively. It was Forkel who, himself a pupil of one of Bach's pupils, and in touch with the esoteric Bach circle in Berlin, paved the way for a new appreciation of Bach in the little book which appeared in 1802 under the title: *The Life, Art and Works of J. S. Bach. For patriotic admirers of genuine musical art.*[1] The work was dedicated to Baron van Swieten. The title and the dedication tell us everything we need to know about the purpose of the book. It was to introduce the German people as such to Bach's work and personality, and with the blessing of the well-known patron of music to rally the lovers of Bach around his banner. The national movement gives the work its background and its aim:

> The preservation of the memory of this great man is an object in which not merely the interest of the art but the honour of the nation itself is deeply involved. . . . This great man . . . was a German. Be proud of him, German fatherland, but be worthy of him too. . . . His works are an invaluable national patrimony with which no other nation has anything to be compared. . . .

[1] *J. S. Bachs Leben, Kunst und Kunstwerke. Für patriotische Verehrer echter musikalischer Kunst.*

—thus the resounding words of the Introduction. It is almost as urgent as the 'Call to my People' (*Aufruf an mein Volk*). Bach is seen as a national hero of the world of music. Forkel plans nothing less than a complete edition of his works. The time was not yet ripe for that, however, and the urgency of the 'summons' faded. But the national idea echoed down the century. For Weber and Richard Wagner, for Max Reger and innumerable writers, the German, the Germanic or Nordic element was predominant in their conception of Bach. That applies even to Wilhelm Dilthey whose magnificent musical impressions, written just before the end of the nineteenth century, were in some respects in advance of musical scholarship, and it continues to appear right up to the present day in the recent studies of Bach by Moser, Steglich, Gurlitt, and others. Like that of the teacher, the contrapuntist, and the organ virtuoso this national element is a perfectly legitimate element in his total character. But it is only one side. There can be no question that Bach's art is thoroughly German, developing and perfecting a combined legacy of the European and the Lutheran spirit by applying to it the methods of a predominantly German tradition. Bach represents the final consummation of the traditional type of characteristically German musician, although he never actually called himself a 'German' nor felt himself a 'German'; it was simply a part of his natural inheritance which he took

39

for granted. What the early Romantics interpreted in him as characteristically 'German' was, fundamentally, his resistance to the dissolving tendencies of the age of rationalist Enlightenment. They saw in him both the guardian of the sacred traditions which they loved so passionately themselves, and the enemy of the rationalist madness from the snares of which they were struggling to make themselves free. In their yearning for the return of a past transfigured by their own wishful thinking and in their despair at the low state of the national fortunes in the present they conjured up this new conception of Bach even before the battle of Jena. Forkel had certainly taken note of the religious element at the heart of Bach's character, but not being a positive believer himself, he was not in a position to re-live the experience in himself. Bach's rootedness in Holy Scripture and Christian dogma, his stubborn orthodoxy, remained a mystery to him. He calls Bach 'devout', 'pious', 'worthy', 'solemn', and refers to the 'sacred style' of his organ works as belonging to the Church; but, on the whole, Forkel does not get any farther than a platitudinous and purely emotional conception of the Christian religion. The fact that he does not even mention the Passions and Cantatas proves that he did not consider them worth mentioning, as he could certainly have had access to them if he had wanted. When it is said that Forkel's new portrait of Bach is hardly less one-sided, hardly less mechanical and lifeless than the old one, we must allow for the fact that he did not intend, as is so often asserted, to write a biography of Bach. What he wrote was more a call to action, a manifesto, a confession of faith. If he had wanted to write a biography he could, owing to his personal contacts with Friedemann and Philipp Emanuel, have had access to a far wider range of material than he actually used in this book. To that extent the criticisms of his work made for instance by the excellent English Bach scholar Sanford Terry are not entirely justified. We have no right to blame him for not giving us a more comprehensive and complete picture of Bach. He could not see beyond the horizon of his own age. No one can do that.

In spite of all his limitations it is Forkel's great merit to have been the first really to break the ice. With his tribute to Bach's memory he carried the name of Bach far beyond the narrow confines of the closed society of the Berlin circle, far beyond the boundaries of the Vienna cognoscenti and the German organist fraternity. The Leipzig *Allgemeine Musikzeitung* could write as early as 1804: 'The resurrection of the dead is taking place in the musical world and fortunately it is confined to the righteous.' Sebastian Bach is mentioned here in the same breath as Philipp Emanuel, Handel, and Jommelli. In this journal Forkel the pioneer was joined by Friedrich Rochlitz, a cultivated Bach exponent and interpreter, Goethe's musical adviser, the pupil of Doles and therefore closely familiar with Bach from an early age. In contrast to Forkel the patriot, he is the purely aesthetic music critic, enjoying this old-fashioned art for its own sake and striving to educate others to understand it. Bach is to his mind the Dürer and Handel the Rubens of German music. The fact that on one occasion he compares Bach with Michaelangelo proves how cultivated was the feeling which he applied to the appreciation of Bach's titanic monumentality. He reveals his feeling for the underlying cosmic order in the works of Bach when in another place he draws a parallel between Bach and Newton. A theologian himself, Rochlitz professed a kind of 'cultural Christianity'; what he valued in Bach, he said, was 'the real Biblical and historical elements, the descriptive and not the merely expressive', which proves that he came close to a genuine appreciation of the very foundations of Bach's music. He himself was, however, too much under the influence of Romantic aestheticism on the one hand, and pietistic rationalism on the other, to understand that Bach is fundamentally concerned with the uncompromising directness of an openly professed faith, with the awful certitude of original sin, with the horrible reality of death and judgement, and with the radiant vision of grace and mercy. Inspired by his own quietistic ideal of piety he transforms Bach, the champion of God, into an enlightened moralist and transposes his monumental images into an atmosphere of calm serenity. He completely fails to appreciate the conflict of daemonic forces in Bach's music, a conflict which Bach depicted with the utmost dramatic reality. By becoming increasingly absorbed in Bach's music Rochlitz did, nevertheless, gradually elaborate an extremely subtle aesthetic interpretation, although the heart and soul of the music eluded him behind the limitations of his own horizon just as it had eluded Forkel.

The patriotic historian Forkel and the Romantic critic Rochlitz were now joined by a third man, Carl Friedrich Zelter, a practical musician who made a decisive mark on the history of Bach in the nineteenth century. Principal of the Berlin Song-Academy founded in 1791, an energetic organizer, a master of the guild of masons, the founder of the Academy of Church and School Music, the only really intimate friend of Goethe in his old age, Zelter was a simple pious character, sober and matter of fact, but capable of enthusiasm and full of life. His correspondence with Goethe is one of the most beautiful in the whole of German literature. He owned an extensive Bach collection which he had inherited from Kirnberger and Agricola from the direct tradition of Friedemann and Philipp Emanuel in Berlin. The father of Zelter's beloved and celebrated pupil, Felix Mendelssohn, had also introduced him to several of Bach's works besides those he owned, for in the Mendelssohn family a good deal of Bach was already being played and Fanny, Felix's sister, knew many of the 'Forty Eight' by heart. Zelter was the first Bach exponent really to know a major part of Bach's vocal works. He knew about 100 of the Cantatas, the two Passions, the *Mass in B minor*, the shorter Masses, the *Magnificat*, and the Motets. He looked upon it as his appointed task to continue the Berlin Bach tradition. He studied motets and cantatas with the Song-Academy, performed chamber and orchestral works with the Academy's orchestral society, though in much-revised arrangements, and performed Bach Motets with the Academy's special choir. 'If I could only let you hear one of Bach's Motets one fine day you would feel in the centre of the world, for they need a man like you to appreciate them at their true worth', he writes to Goethe in 1827. He did not think it feasible to perform the Passions and Cantatas, however. He tried them out with a small audience of friends but never performed them in public. In 1811 and 1813 he rehearsed the *Mass in B minor* and, in 1815, fourteen years before Mendelssohn's performance, the *St. Matthew Passion*. Bach's passionate dramatic feeling and mystic ecstasy meant little, however, to his sober rationalistic mind.

The biggest obstacle is the atrocious German chorale texts which are full of the polemical earnestness of the Reformation and try to disturb the mind of the non-believer by smoking him out with the dense fumes of belief, which is what no one really wants nowadays.

He revised and smoothed out the texts and the music as well, simplifying the polyphony and the instrumentation, which he regarded merely as a matter of fashion.

Old Bach with all his originality is a son of his age and could not escape French influence. We can, however, dissociate him from this foreign element, it comes off like thin froth and the shining contents lie immediately beneath. Consequently I have arranged several of his church compositions, solely for my own pleasure, and my heart tells me that old Bach nods approval, just as the worthy Haydn used to say 'Yes, yes, that was what I wished.' -

In his reply Goethe puts the critical question:

You might give me a serious exposition of what you call the French froth which you take it upon yourself to separate from the basic German element, and somehow or other reveal this instructive relationship to my outer and inner senses.

Evading the question Zelter has to admit in his reply: 'What I called the French froth in Bach is—like the air, omnipresent, but intangible.' Zelter was a man of direct unpremeditated views, like Goethe in that respect, and what drew him so instinctively to Bach was probably quite simply the overwhelming elemental musical force, the full-blooded energy which beats through all the veins of Bach's music. He did not succeed, however, in becoming clear in his own mind about the roots of this elemental force. He could not see that Bach's

style was the full and adequate expression of his orthodox convictions and ever-present dogmatic beliefs, and
that every alteration of the words and the music must
inevitably distort the underlying meaning. To that
extent his vision was subject to the same limitations
as that of Forkel and Rochlitz. But he was superior to
them inasmuch as he was one of the most fearless
stalwarts who have ever championed the master by
the practical performance of his music. He summed
up his views on Bach in the magnificent words of a
letter written to Goethe in 1827:

Everything considered which might be held against him,
this Leipzig cantor is a divine phenomenon, clear, yet inexplicable. I could cry out to him: 'thou gavest me a task to do,
and I have brought thee to light again'.

But he did not fully understand Bach. His ardent
love and passionate spirit of adventure and discovery
came up against an insuperable barrier in Bach's religious faith and after the most honest attempts to
understand it he gave up the struggle altogether.

In one way, however, Zelter did indirectly surpass
the achievement of his two fellow Bach exponents. He
was instrumental in introducing the greatest German
mind of the nineteenth century to Bach and thereby
revealing to him what he had long sought after, the
innermost spirit of music. In May 1821, when he was
twelve years old, Zelter's pupil, Felix Mendelssohn,
was Goethe's guest in Weimar for ten days and played

Bach to him every morning and evening. In his robust and free and easy style Zelter had told Goethe what he thought about Bach. Goethe had listened carefully and when he was staying in Bad Berka with the mayor and organist Schütz he lay in bed and had Bach played to him. 'Bach is like that, he must be listened to in quietness of spirit.' Such listening led Goethe's universal mind to an intuitive understanding of Bach. He hardly knew any of the vocal music; the performance of the *St. Matthew Passion* in 1829 he only heard in spirit by reading Zelter's account of it: 'It was as if I heard the tumult of the sea roaring from afar.' If he had known the Cantatas and the Passions the dogmatic Christianity of all these works would probably have meant little to him. But from his knowledge of the keyboard works, the organ movements, and the Chorale Preludes he became profoundly aware of the significance of Bach's work as the incarnation of the spirit of the universe.

It was there in Berka when my mind was in a state of perfect composure and free from external distractions that I first obtained some idea of your grand master. I said to myself, it is as if the eternal harmony were conversing within itself as it may have done in the bosom of God just before the creation of the world. So likewise did it move in my inmost soul and it seemed as if I neither possessed nor needed ears, nor any other sense—least of all the eyes.

That is the record of an historical moment of the

first order: the most universal mind apprehending, with no preconceptions, simply through his direct personal experience of Bach, the secret of music which he had struggled to fathom all his life. Goethe's readiness to open his mind and spirit to the music of Bach is symbolic of Bach's emergence in the German people and the whole world. Goethe himself set the seal on the experience vouchsafed to his receptive spirit in the little-known verses which he inscribed in 1818 in one of the volumes of Bach belonging to the organist Schütz.

Let me hear and let me feel what the music speaks to the heart: let it give me warmth and light in the cool days of life. The senses are always open to new experience when something great is offered to them, something that, original and imperishable, shrinks not from the critic's gaze, and with life drawn from the depths, joins the heavenly choir and builds a new world for us, unforced and independently. When the disciple presents himself before his master, may it be for praiseworthy gain. For the nearness of pure spirits purifies the open mind.

It would probably be going too far to assume that Goethe's later conversion from pantheism to a belief in the transcendence of the Divine was partly determined by his experience of Bach, but it does seem certain that the conversion and the experience were in harmonious accord with each other.

It was by forgoing the direction of the first revival of the *St. Matthew Passion* in favour of Mendelssohn, however, that Zelter did his greatest service to the cause of Bach. 'Felix rehearsed the music under me and will conduct it, for which purpose I am passing my chair over to him.' On 11 March 1829, a hundred years after its composition, the Berlin Song-Academy performed the work which had been slumbering in silence for roughly eighty years. It was an event of incalculable significance. Together with Goethe's recognition of his greatness it marks the fundamental turning-point in the history of Bach.

Mendelssohn was closely familiar with Bach's works from his home, from Zelter's training, and from the Berlin tradition. In 1823 Zelter, otherwise the grimly jealous guardian of his treasures, had given permission for a copy of the *St. Matthew Passion* to be made for Mendelssohn, and in 1827 Mendelssohn rehearsed the work. Zelter considered the actual performance of the work an impossibility. The general public, used to the ingratiating tones of Graun's *Death of Jesus* and not willing to have its sentimental taste disturbed, considered Bach dry and unintelligible. Mendelssohn himself held back at first from this attempt to revolutionize the musical traditions of Berlin. Finally convinced, he is reported by the 'stage-player', Eduard Devrient, as saying: 'Well, it needs a stage-player and a Jew boy to reintroduce the greatest Christian music to the people.' Eduard Devrient, the 'comic actor', was Mendelssohn's friend and the real driving force behind the enterprise. He was the first to sing the part of Christ in the Passion. The public was deeply moved by the first performance. 'A mood of solemn consecration', 'genuine religious emotion', 'soulful feeling', are some of the impressions recorded at the time. Hegel was present and began to catch a glimpse of Bach's greatness. 'One felt the epoch-making results which would flow from this revival of the popular influence of a half-forgotten genius', writes Devrient. And Hegel speaks of 'Bach's grand, truly Protestant, robust and so to speak erudite genius which we have only recently learned again to appreciate at its full value'. The spell was broken. At one blow, Bach's name had come into its own at last. The amazing fact is that with the practical performance of this work there came an understanding of Bach as the champion of religion. Thus were the labours of Forkel, Rochlitz, Zelter, and Mendelssohn brought to fruition at last. Slowly at first but then more quickly and with ever-increasing intensity and speed the stream of the Bach tradition widened and deepened. By the turn of the century the stream had developed into a surging torrent. The posthumous life and fruitful influence of Bach were secure.

What passed as Bach's work in the first performance of the *St. Matthew Passion* was still far removed from the original score. Zelter's 'French froth' had its after-effect. Even though Mendelssohn, as we know to-day, did not use Zelter's score, his own arrangement was no less a travesty of Bach's intentions. A complete performance of the work was not considered feasible, so a compromise was worked out to suit the requirements of public taste. An attempt was made 'to make the antiquated work modern, vivid and alive by carefully selecting the most appropriate means to this end', as Eduard Devrient puts it. Big cuts were made, the scoring altered, the rough edges of the arias polished down; in fact, only the introductions of some of the arias were allowed to stand at all, the phrasing was changed, and the expression highly charged with Romantic emotionalism. To us to-day the *St. Matthew Passion* in this shape would sound like a caricature of its true self, but to dress it up in the style of the 1830's was probably the concession that had inevitably to be made in order to secure a hearing for it in pre-1848 Berlin. Gratified by its success, Devrient asserted that the arrangement 'seems to have been right, as it has been used in most of the later performances of the work'.

The cultural background of this epoch-making turning-point in the history of Bach's reputation was the Berlin of the years following the Wars of Liberation, the Berlin of the early Romantic movement, of Hoffmann and Weber, the Berlin of the Humboldts and the new university, of the new historical learning and the religious revival movement. Great as were the

efforts made by August Eberhard Müller, the Cantor
of St. Thomas's, to reintroduce Bach's Cantatas
in Leipzig, under his successor Schicht the active
interest in Bach faded out again, although Schicht performed useful service as a collector of Bach Cantata
scores. In Frankfurt J. Nepomuk Schelbe founded
the 'St. Cecilia Society' in 1818, which subsequently
developed a lively interest in Bach; in 1822 he met the
thirteen-year-old Mendelssohn and had some influence on him; in 1828 he gave a first performance of
the Credo from the *Mass in B minor* and a number of
Bach Cantatas. In Zürich H. G. Nägeli tried to publish some of Bach's works from the rich stores of his
personal library, but did not get very far. Hoffmeister
and Kühnel, Breitkopf and Härtel in Leipzig, Koll-
mann in London, and a few music publishers in
Vienna printed a number of Bach's instrumental
works. But all these efforts were only a small beginning. The only place where a thorough-going Bach
revival could begin was Berlin, the Berlin where
Weber was breaking Spontini's monopoly; where
E. T. A. Hoffmann was enraptured by the first performance of the *Freischütz* in 1821; where men like
Arndt, Stein, and Fichte had kindled German nationa-
list feelings; where the playing of Paganini in 1829 in
the very same year as the first performance of the *St.
Matthew Passion* had made the public aware of the
daemonic side of Romantic music; where Rellstab

and Adolf Bernhard Marx were calling attention to the titanic element in the genius of Beethoven; and where, finally, the new arrival of Biblical fundamentalism and pietism had aroused wide sections of the population including the nobility, the artisan class, business people, and students to a deeply felt experience of a Romantically exuberant religiousness. The Enlightenment had come to an end in Berlin as early as 1815, and by the close of the 1820's the victory of neo-pietism was an assured fact. 'Interior conflicts with God again became a matter of human experience' (Karl Holl). Although Schleiermacher stood aside, the number of theologians and non-theologians in whom a new experience of Christianity and a new seriousness made themselves felt was overwhelming. Court society, particularly the Crown Prince, who pressed for repeated performances of the *St. Matthew Passion*, led the way. In this new intellectual, national, spiritual, and religious awakening the world of Bach was newly understood and in this rediscovered musical world the yearning of a whole generation attained a vivid reality and realization.

Breslau was the only other city where conditions were comparable to those prevailing in Berlin. In that city J. Theodor Mosevius, the founder and conductor of the Breslau Song-Academy, became the leader of the Bach movement. Carl von Winterfeld was another active force, a judge of the High Court by profession, but at the same time a fine musician and the first historian of Protestant Church music, whose work on *The Evangelical Hymn* remains fundamental to-day in some respects. Mosevius was present at the Berlin performance of the *St. Matthew Passion* in 1829 and, though it is true that he could not follow the choral fantasia 'O man, bewail thy grievous sin' which concludes the first part, the work as a whole moved him deeply, and only a year later he performed it in Breslau. Later on he penetrated more deeply into Bach's mind and spirit than Zelter and Mendelssohn. In his writings on the Bach Cantatas, of which he performed a whole series, he proves himself to be a man of deep faith and genuine Lutheran outlook. The religious revival movement was a living experience for him as it was for the whole of Breslau. Winterfeld's house was the centre of the movement in Breslau and the Breslau Song-Academy started there too. Breslau was also one of the chief centres of national patriotism: the 'Call to my People' had gone out from this city and here men like Hippel, Stein, Hardenberg, Scharnhorst, Steffens, and others had prepared the revival of Prussia. Here, too, Bach's Passion fell, as in Berlin, on the most fertile soil. Next to Berlin Breslau was the strongest centre of the new Bach movement. It was here, too, that the two main trends in the restoration of Evangelical Church music which dominated for so long, and in fact in some ways still dominate, the practical side of

Church music, began to go their separate ways. The first was the specifically Protestant and Romantic Bach movement, which saw in Bach the musical embodiment of Lutheranism and therefore wanted to reintroduce his works and subsequently those of his contemporaries, as well as Baroque music in general, into the services of the Church. The other trend was the Purist movement, with an inter-denominational Classical ideal of 'pure' Church music which it found embodied in Palestrina and in the whole a-cappella style of the Roman school. In the Catholic Church this latter trend produced the so-called Cecilian movement and found a leading representative in the Heidelberg Professor of Law, Justus Thibaut, the author of the famous treatise *On the Purity of Music*.[1] Thibaut also studied Bach Motets with his choral society, because they were regarded as a-cappella music, but he failed to reconcile himself to the Passions and Cantatas and regarded them as fundamentally not Church music at all. In Breslau it was Winterfeld who, although a glowing admirer of Bach, considered his Church music to be not sufficiently popular, too intellectualized, too exacting, too realistic, and too passionate for use in the services of the Church. In fact, difficult as it was for him to make the decision, he prevented the *St. Matthew Passion* and the Cantatas from being performed in church. Once again, a temporary

[1] *Über Reinheit der Tonkunst.*

conception of the nature of religion determined the current view of Bach. The age had broken loose from dogmatic religion and was unable to grasp the dogmatic depths of Bach's work. The limitations which were supposed to be characteristic of Bach were, in fact, fundamentally only the limitations of the age itself.

Königsberg, the third city where the *St. Matthew Passion* was performed, is proof, if proof were needed, of the fact that all the conditions mentioned above had to be fulfilled to give the impulse to a thorough-going Bach movement. There was no lack of patriotism here, no lack of historical feeling, nor any lack of the intense Romantic emotionalism which was felt here as everywhere else in Germany. But there was no religious background in Königsberg. Rationalism still continued to hold sway here for many years. The revival movement in the Church was frowned on and when the *St. Matthew Passion* was performed here for the first time in 1832, some of the congregation ran out of the church even during the first half. Others criticized the work as 'out-of-date rubbish'. This 'greatest Christian music', as Mendelssohn had called the *Passion*, met with no response and the Bach movement fell on barren soil.

Despite all the setbacks, however, the rivulets of the older Bach tradition had developed in the first half of the nineteenth century into a strong though narrow mountain torrent still meeting many an obstacle, and the conceptions of Bach had become transformed and deepened. No matter what each individual saw in Bach, no matter how broad or narrow the individual understanding of him, one thing had emerged from all these activities. Bach as an historical phenomenon and as an active influence had become a problem for discussion and research. That his work concealed a world of previously unsuspected wealth, that this enigmatic figure must have been rooted in a world to which access had been lost, that he was not merely a teacher and father of organists, a calculating theorist and constructor of fugues, but that rather in him the whole force of a lost vitality was erupting into the light of day, so much had been learnt at least. It was natural, therefore, that he should attract the attention of historians. In order properly to study him at all, however, it was first necessary to obtain reliable information about his work and its historical foundations. Exactly 100 years after Bach's death the mountain torrent widens into a stream and divides in two directions. The one tributary sets the mills of historical research moving, the other stimulates the collection and publication of the complete works.

Almost the only part of Bach's work that had been made available so far was the organ and keyboard works. Attempts to publish the vocal works had failed owing to the apathy of the public. The *Magnificat* was first printed in 1811, and the *Mass in A* in 1818, but hardly any notice was taken of either of them. In 1821 Breitkopf and Härtel produced as the first cantata to be published *Ein' feste Burg*, but Zelter had to report to Goethe in 1829 that the work would have to be 'classed as a white elephant'. The *St. Matthew Passion* was published in 1830 and the *St. John Passion* in 1831. The *Mass in B minor* was not published in full for the first time until 1845, ninety-five years after Bach's death and about 110 years after it was composed. It was clear that by themselves the publishers would never manage a complete edition of Bach's works. Robert Schumann, a Bach enthusiast and a man with historical interests, called on the nation, in his journal of 1837, to undertake the task as Forkel had done thirty-five years before, and shortly after the foundation of the English Handel Society in 1843 he was able to announce that the plan for a complete edition of Bach would soon be put before the public. The Bach Gesellschaft was founded at last in 1850, sponsored by Moritz Hauptmann, Otto Jahn, Karl Ferdinand Becker, and Robert Schumann. Mosevius and Winterfeld also took a lively interest in it. From 1859 onwards the excellent scholar, Wilhelm Rust, took over chief editorial responsibility. Later on the older men were replaced by men like Dörffel, Graf Waldersee, Ernst Naumann, Franz Wüllner, and Philipp Spitta. Without the energetic support of

Franz Liszt and the self-sacrificing enthusiasm of many practical musicians the completion of the work would have been impossible. Only a few people fully appreciated the importance of the undertaking. One of the few was Brahms, who once described as the two greatest events in his life the founding of the German Reich and the completion of the Bach Gesellschaft edition of Bach's works. Those whom it really concerned most of all, the Church and Church music organizations, remained completely indifferent. In 1900 the edition was concluded with Volume 46. Now at last, exactly 150 years after Bach's death, the German people and the whole world had full access to his work. It is true, of course, that knowledge of the sources had grown considerably in the meantime. Much was proved to be no longer tenable, revisions and rearrangments had to be undertaken. To-day the time would have been ripe for the production of an entirely new edition of Bach's complete works, if the distress and impoverishment of the times and the loss of very many of the sources had not withdrawn from the German people all prospect and possibility of such an undertaking.

The complete edition of Bach's works was an achievement of incalculable significance. It not only became the gateway to a new understanding, to an historical correction and deepening of the accepted ideas of Bach, to a new and glorious chapter in musical research in general, but it also inspired a surprising advance in practical music making. It inspired also a new interest in the music of the other masters of the age of the Baroque and the rediscovery of the whole of the older music; in fact it stimulated all modern research into musical sources to a much greater extent than Chrysander's complete edition of Handel, which, appearing at the same time as the Bach edition, failed to direct the attention of musicians and scholars to anything but Handel himself. All the innumerable recent complete editions of the old masters, the great serial publications, the editions of the *Denkmäler Deutscher Tonkunst* are indebted to the Bach edition in one way or another. It also gave a powerful stimulus to the study of the practical problems involved in the performance of the older music. All the efforts of the last fifty years devoted to the revival of the old instruments and the authentic performance of the music were all ultimately inspired by the Bach edition. But this epoch-making achievement has also had immense influence in the sphere of composition. Which of the great composers from Schumann to Reger, from Mendelssohn to Strauss and Pfitzner, from Brahms to Wagner, and from Bruckner to Verdi has not somewhere been deeply influenced by the complete edition of the works of Bach? It opened the sluice through which his art and technique, as well as his mind and faith, poured into the creative work of the neo-Romantics and neo-Classicists. The *Rosen-kavalier* is as inconceivable without this influence as Mendelssohn's *St. Paul*, the *Mastersingers*, the *German Requiem*, Reger's *Hiller Variations*, or Bruckner's masses and symphonies. For the first time in history creative minds in music experienced the overwhelming influence of past greatness so profoundly that it set the whole direction and standard for their own work. An epoch-making change took place in the half-century covered by the Bach edition, since for the first time European music was seen as part of a definite historical process. Musical historians began to interpret Bach as the centre of gravity of the whole history of music. Wagner saw in Bach 'the history of the innermost life of the German spirit during the cruel century in which the German people were completely blotted out'. Brahms declared that it would grieve him if the whole of music, the works of Schubert, Schumann, and Beethoven were to disappear, but that he would be utterly inconsolable if he were to be deprived of Bach. Reger called him 'the beginning and end of all music', and Beethoven had already declared 'He ought not to be called Bach [brook] but ocean'. It is still impossible to estimate the full significance of this irruption of Bach into the musical world of the nineteenth century as an historical event. It is, indeed, an event without parallel in the whole of history and it has transformed the musical world from the very depths.

If the mere appearance of Bach's complete works alone had such a revolutionary effect on the whole world of music, practical and creative alike, the results of the Bach research which began its course so impressively during the same period deepened both the knowledge of Bach and his influence. For the first time the Bach problem became the subject of historical research. C. L. Hilgenfeldt undertook a first evaluation (*J. S. Bach's Life, Influence and Works*, 1850)[1] with inadequate knowledge of the sources. This was soon followed in 1865 by the first comprehensive study by C. H. Bitter, and from then on the books on Bach came thick and fast. In the fifty years between 1800 and 1850 only thirty-seven books on Bach appeared, all of them small and mostly quite unimportant; from 1850 to 1900 there were 163, amongst them a number of large-scale works; in the ten years from 1900 to 1910 alone no less than 297 appeared. Bitter not only succeeded to an amazing extent in uncovering the sources of Bach's life and personality, he was the first Bach scholar to undertake an outline of Bach based on genuine historical criticism. Criticized unfavourably and unjustly by Spitta ten years later, Bitter's achievement has been quite undeservedly neglected right up to the present day. This highly cultivated, conscientious, and brilliantly intelligent Prussian Finance Minister was the first to try to

[1] *J. S. Bachs Leben, Wirken und Werke.*

appreciate Bach entirely from the religious and ecclesiastical point of view. The still widely held conception of Bach as a jealous guardian of tradition committed exclusively to the Church and her ordinances, composing solely 'for the honour of God, for religious edification, and for the benefit of his fellow-citizens' goes back to him. He regards the secular and instrumental works as a mere by-product, a compromise, and the Cöthen years and Bach's ambitions as a Hofkapellmeister seem to him to be an inexplicable mystery or else simply 'a blemish'. Bitter failed to see that Bach was a human being full of human contradictions, inner conflicts, and wavering decisions, that he stood on the verge of a turning-point in history, that he fought out in a full and active life the battle between inclination and duty, between the demands of his own age and an historical mission of which he was painfully conscious, and that his final decision in favour of a world declining towards its close was both an act of enormous renunciation and a monumental deed. Bitter interprets Bach's work as specifically Christian and Lutheran without finding in it more than a religious atmosphere. He strips off the aesthetic emotionalism indulged in by the neo-pietists and forgoes the stage-effects of patriotic and Romantic propaganda. He keeps to the historical facts and discovers the roots of Bach in the soil of an entirely unpietistic orthodox piety. He came close there to a true understanding of one of Bach's basic qualities. But by regarding this piety of Bach's as 'simple' and unproblematical, by considering him, to put it somewhat crudely, as a model of ecclesiastical submissiveness, he shut his eyes to the decisive fact that Bach was immersed in all the waters of an age-old dogmatism and scholasticism and was not simply expressing moods in his music but expounding all the complicated problems of the old-orthodox interpretation of the Bible. Thus his exposition of Bach amounted in the last analysis to little more than an affectionate but prosaic portrait of the master with little relation to the actual work which he achieved.

Philipp Spitta drew from incomparably deeper sources for his study of Bach which appeared in 1873 and 1879 and which is still justifiably considered the classic biography of Bach. We are not concerned here with the general importance of his work as a contribution to the history of music: it was an unparalleled achievement. For the first time Bach as an historical figure was seen against the background of a whole century of German music which Spitta was himself the first to explore. Bach is here no longer the solitary hero of the musical world, the meteor fallen from the sky, but the organic product of a long historical development. Spitta reveals him as the final product of historical conditions on the one hand and as rising from ecclesiastical and religious foundations on the other.

Spitta was not concerned, however, with another question which interests us to-day, the social structure as the creative artist's native soil. The religious life of his own parsonage home had progressed from a Romantic type of emotional Christianity through the neo-pietist revival to Fundamentalism and a new, strictly denominational Lutheranism, a kind of neo-orthodoxy. The father, J. Philipp Spitta, was the author of *Psalter and Harp*. A strictly practised Lutheranism was the vital atmosphere of the home as it had been the atmosphere of Bach's home, and this background of common experience made it possible for Spitta to understand Bach very closely. It gave his biography the warmth of an appreciation based on common personal experience. First of all, Bach's life is placed in the wide context of family and local origins, of craft and traditional background. The artistic pedigree of the Bach musicians is established (though it needs revising to-day) and Bach's humanity is then portrayed in all its power and dignity. The mechanical perfection of Bitter's portrait is abandoned and the real character and inevitability of the human being are revealed. If Spitta cannot be wholly absolved of adding a little extra colour to the picture, and if, as one must admit, he often idealizes his hero at the expense of his predecessors, contemporaries, and successors, such weaknesses must be put down partly to the general Romantic glorification of great men which was current at the time and partly to the topical controversies of the years when he was writing. For at the time the last of those embittered conflicts was raging, which, running through whole centuries, have brought new life and energy into music. It was the quarrel between Classicism and neo-Germanism, between Hanslick and Brahms on the one side and Wagner, Liszt, and Bruckner on the other. There could be no doubt as to which side Spitta was on. As he saw it, Bach had to be adapted to the purity of the Classical ideal. If his portrait of Bach thereby lost something of the full-bloodedness of real life, it gained by its unflinching acknowledgement of the fact that Bach stands or falls with orthodox Lutheranism and dogmatic religious faith. Spitta saw deeper than Bitter. He was also the first to see the conflict between orthodoxy and pietism which took place in Bach. The fact that he greatly underestimated the pietist element and that he, too, saw in Bach a character of pure unclouded piety means that his picture lacks the immense variety of contradictory and complementary features of the original Bach, whose complexity is, indeed, well-nigh unfathomable. All the contradictions and complexities are smoothed out with an all too efficiently laid on varnish. Spitta was dimly aware of the many problems but he did not really see them. Instead of problems, we have the purity and gentleness of a self-sufficing perfection and the smoothness and unalloyed simplicity of pious resignation.

Spitta recognized the fighting, doubting, struggling, and victorious Bach in the biographical part but not in the critical part of his work. The life and work are not presented in full harmony and it is no solution of the contradiction when Spitta describes Bach as building his own private world away from everyday reality. That is a fundamentally wrong approach. With every fibre of his being Bach lived in the reality of this present world. But 'reality' and 'the world' were for him what had become no more than a spectre for most of his contemporaries, namely, original sin and damnation, death and the devil. The fact that for long stretches in Spitta's work our view of the leading figure is often hidden by the abundance of historical detail is not merely a literary defect but suggests that Spitta himself had not completely mastered the complexity of the historical problems involved. There are gaps between the ideal and the reality which he fills with flowery poetical descriptions.

The drawback of Spitta's truly colossal work was that by his subjective and emotional descriptions he unintentionally and unwittingly gave rise to an extravagantly over-poetic misinterpretation of Bach's character, which continues even to-day to silt up the clear stream of genuine Bach research and has sentimentalized and degraded the popular conception of Bach *ad nauseam*. Difficult as it was to surpass Spitta's achievement, even to add anything essential to it, the weeds of the cheapest sentimental adoration shot up all the more abundantly. To graze on the pastures of the great is a cheap and easy pastime. In place of the long since recognized problems, in place of Lutheran, racial, and national or simply historical factors as the groundwork of his character, Bach was either praised to the skies or reduced to the level of a middle-class Philistine, and the result was often sheer rubbish. An almost incredible tendency to use Bach as material for fancy pictures after the style of the cheap novel and popular film came to replace the historical truth, even influencing expositions intended to be taken seriously; plays and imaginary diaries dripping with senti-mentality distorted the conception of Bach held by vast numbers of people. Snobbish aesthetes began to swagger about apparently thinking they had a perfect right completely to ignore the basic facts established by Bitter and Spitta, and they included scholars like Jadassohn and Alfred Heuss, journalists like Richard Batka, Gustav Doempke, and Karl Storck, whilst even conscientious musicologists like Pirro, Wolfrum, and Hubert Parry were not able to escape their influence entirely. It was a dangerous tendency. It removed Bach from both the national and the ecclesiastical soil which after all had fostered his development, from the tradition of technical skill, and from the historical depths in which his character was rooted. Under the influence of a mistaken liberalistic outlook, they

68

believed that Bach had mostly followed his own genius in his work, and that his Church and home locality, his faith and belief in dogma, his family and his craft were simply unavoidable restrictions on the artistic freedom of a great personality. Angry indignation was expressed at his supposed servility to aristocratic patrons and at the humiliation he received at the hands of the clergy, which were alleged to have acted as shackles on his natural genius. They refused to see that these were in fact the natural elements in which his life was grounded, which he accepted absolutely, and which he even struggled ardently to maintain against the dissolving tendencies of the age. Against all the facts Bach was turned into a homeless refugee, an aimless and restless titan. Uprooted as this age of exaggerated individualism was itself, it dragged the great man down to its own level, robbing him of the very roots which had fed his whole life and work. The theological critics of this tendency, men like Julius Smend and Friedrich Spitta, Georg Rietschel and Max Herold, were unable to enforce their views against the snobbish aesthetes because, free thinking and sentimental, inclined to compromise and out of date in their views on music as they were, they themselves were far from any deep understanding of Bach, and because they failed in addition at precisely the point where they ought to and could have exerted an active influence, namely, in the infusion of Bach's

69

music into the services of the Church. No attempt was made even to undertake a thorough scientific study of Bach from the theological point of view, and the Evangelical church has still to pay a debt of honour in this respect. If the journalistic portrait of Bach at the close of the nineteenth and beginning of the twentieth centuries became more and more vague and lifeless, the portrait drawn by the theologians became increasingly pale and colourless.

These conflicting and to some extent destructive tendencies in the history of Bach can probably best be understood as reactions to the enormously constructive influence and inspiration which had flowed from the Bach Gesellschaft edition into the general musical life of the time. But this widespread influence had another undesirable result. Zelter and Mendelssohn, Schelble and Mosevius had already led the way in believing in the necessity of adapting Bach to the needs of their own environment, of modernizing him and painting him over with the colours of their own age. The second half of the century cheerfully carried on the 'good work'. Bach's works appeared in innumerable different editions, touched up and revised, falsified and smartened up with all the clever showiness of late Romantic orchestral, choral, and instrumental techniques. They became the playground for self-important virtuosos and vain conductors. Even to-day, one can still find in most musical homes and

even in the libraries of music teachers, choir conductors, and chamber musicians editions which flout
all standards of honesty and truthfulness. In this respect the Neue Bach Gesellschaft, which was founded
in 1900 after the old society had completed its work
with the conclusion of the complete edition, has done
nothing to improve matters; on the contrary, it has
made things worse by supporting with all the prestige
of its authority the performance of Bach by massed
choirs, with orchestral effects à la Mahler and with all
the pianistic and vocal antics of the professional virtuoso, all of which is an accurate reflection of the popular
journalistic conception of Bach. Only in the last few
decades has anything been done to remedy this state
of affairs and so far only the beginnings of success have
been achieved in this truly herculean purge. The mass
of well-intentioned but inaccurate and distorting
editions of Bach produced by men like Robert Franz,
Felix Mottl, Carl Czerny, Ferdinand David, and innumerable others, the uninspired and dishonest performances of Bach's works which are still given
even to-day, the hair-raising absurdities perpetrated
even by such masters as Reger and Busoni, all these
things only prove how intrinsically hollow must
have been the conception of Bach which led to such
travesties.

If we are seriously concerned to establish a more
conscientious and authentic standard in our approach

71

to Bach then we have to pay an enormous debt of accumulated guilt.

In this period of such divergent tendencies, of detailed scholarly research and consolidation on the one hand and the watering down of Bach's works by the dilettante and practical musicians on the other, Wilhelm Dilthey was the first to seek and find in his Bach improvisations, which were written before 1900 but not published until 1933, the way to a deeper conception of Bach quite independently of the controversies of the day. Nietzsche had already preceded him, not establishing any firm relationship to Bach but illuminating his work with occasional flashes of insight. In the *St. Matthew Passion* he heard again 'the completely forgotten Christian religion proclaimed with all the power of a Gospel', and in Bach's music in general he found 'the denial of the will without any suggestion of asceticism'. He makes that comment in order to contrast Bach with Wagner who, although the bases of his art were purely aesthetic, 'crawled to the Cross' in Parsifal. To say, as Nietzsche does on another occasion, that Bach 'stands on the threshold of European music' is an error based on lack of historical knowledge, but, on the other hand, to say that he 'looked back to the middle ages' was, like so much in Nietzsche, a magnificent piece of intuition, despite his ignorance of the historical facts.

Dilthey sees Bach in a line with Dante and Giotto,

'in fact they lag behind him because only music can be wholly successful in raising the religious consciousness into the sphere of eternity'. Dilthey is the first to appreciate Bach the mystic, the descendant and contemporary of the mystics and pietists Gerhard and Spee. According to him, religious experience was expressed directly and absolutely in Bach's music, the much-criticized libretti were merely unessential links between the experience and the music. He sees that this music expresses every single religious idea, gives the fullest possible direct expression to the ultimate polarities, the 'coincidentia oppositorum' in the Christian consciousness itself, and expresses an 'understanding of the ultimate depths of the religious world'. Dilthey also had a much more full-blooded conception of Bach's personality than the faint-hearted biographers who were writing at the same time; he calls him 'a violent man' with whom it was very difficult to live.

Dilthey's promising contribution to a new understanding of Bach was not published for forty years. But in 1905 Albert Schweitzer's book on Bach, probably the best known of all books on Bach to-day, although it is now as out of date as it is dangerous, broke into the sultry atmosphere of the time like a cleansing thunder-storm. If Spitta's achievement had been the result of assiduous historical research and personal religious experience, Schweitzer's was based on the intuitions of a highly gifted mind. He adds nothing to

73

Spitta, either historically or biographically, in fact in scholarly equipment he lags a long way behind him. But he drew from a deep personal experience of Bach's art and was able to expound this experience in a brilliant but at the same time simple and thoughtful style. The wealth of practical experience on which the book is based is amazing for such a young man. He was only thirty when the book was written. Schweitzer did not actually open up any new lines of inquiry. His treatment was exclusively aesthetic, in fact he deliberately put aesthetics in the place of history, regarding the historians' work on Bach as already completed. But he followed the line of aesthetic inquiry with so much intuitive understanding and so consistently that his interpretation has had important influence and results. He discovered in Bach the great designer and painter, whose whole language has to be understood as an interpretation of words in sound. He elaborated a theory of thematic motives in Bach which forms as it were a musical vocabulary corresponding to the verbal vocabulary, in which pain and joy, falling and striding, life and death, darkness and light are expressed in terms of sound. With an unparalleled power of intuition and with no previous historical knowledge he saw all this in Bach about thirty years before musicologists began to discover its application to the work of the whole period of the Baroque. On the basis of this theory he sees the whole of Bach's art as essentially expressionistic, 'simply a continuous chain of violent convulsions'. If that is in fact Bach's procedure then it proves to Schweitzer's mind that his methods are psychological and that he can only be understood psychologically. Just as in *Tristan* Wagner expresses varying spiritual moods with every twist and turn of the Leitmotif, so in the same way does Bach, who is fundamentally anything but a classical artist, but rather a representational artist depicting spiritual facts and situations in his music, a writer of programme-music, far removed from all conventions and traditions. Bach's capacity in this field is based on his personal religion. With the prophet's power of divination he penetrates to the inner spirit of the objects he is representing, he is a mystic, an ecstatic, and a prophet (this is also Dilthey's interpretation, of whose work Schweitzer was, of course, unaware at the time). Such an artist cannot, however, have been (as Spitta makes him out to be) simply a quiet, religiously-minded family man and a worthy citizen. Schweitzer discovers Bach the fighter, discovers the unruly violence of his temperament, the force and dogmatism of 'the thunderer'. This conception of Bach is full of life and close to earth, yet art and life have still not been brought into perfect unity. If Spitta had not been able to settle the alleged conflict between Bach's life and his work, Schweitzer simply bridged the gap by declaring that in the process of creative work the giant became transformed into a pious recluse and in the seclusion of his retreat the overwhelming energy of his nature poured itself into the creation of musical images. Bach's technique of composition is, according to Schweitzer, 'no longer simply a technique, but an interpretation of the world, an image of Being', and Bach's polyphony is a 'manifestation of the original creative power which is revealed in the infinity of the concentric revolving spheres. The tremendous power of his creative mind makes us tremble more than that of Kant or Hegel. His music is a phenomenon of the reality of the inconceivable as is the cosmos itself.' Art in itself is religion. Art, religion, form, and expression all blended into one are the most direct expression of the power of mystical insight. Creativity is simply the emanation of religious thought. The style, the form, and the method all flow from this one source.

The strength and the weakness of Schweitzer's exposition are obvious. Its strength lies in its consistency and the personal experience on which it is based, its weakness in the purely aesthetic approach. At one and the same time one can follow Schweitzer with enthusiastic assent and yet decide against him historically. He fails to see the complexity of Bach's personal religion, he thinks of him as a genius striving to cast off the fetters of his own age, like an eagle in a cage. The ties which bind him to his ancestry and nation, his rootedness in traditional musical conceptions, and in the faith and dogma of the Church, are merely incidental qualities. What he is concerned with is essentially the isolated artistic phenomenon of Bach as such. Schweitzer sees him rather as a genius of universal humanity, with no limitations and the soil in which he is rooted more a coincidence than a necessity. From this point of view Schweitzer's conception of Bach shares the limitations of the age in which it was written. The more we advance beyond the fluctuating ground of a purely aesthetic evaluation of Bach the more inadequate Schweitzer's work as a whole seems to us. What remains unchanged is the impression of a vividly portrayed human being and the insight into the pictorial methods of Bach's style. The artistic and historical figure portrayed by Schweitzer faded, however, under the impact of the revolutionary changes of the following decade.

The First World War came and with it and after it a far-reaching spiritual transformation of the German people. The more conscious people became of the relativity of the old artistic standards, the clearer it became that neither the historical nor the religious and aesthetic standards that had been previously applied to Bach were any longer adequate. No one had ever reached the heart of the matter and probed the question of the nature of Bach's innermost spirit. What was to be done about it? It is characteristic of

the situation that had now arisen that a new seriousness was applied to efforts to approach Bach from the
practical side. In this direction it was particularly the
younger generation after the war who gathered round
Bach with a new sense of responsibility and in a spirit
of clear-headed devotion to his work. In their efforts
to play Bach in a style of severe simplicity far removed
from all the dazzling virtuosity of the past, and all
the vanity of so-called 'interpretations', they may have
sometimes shot beyond the mark. But by striving to
re-establish as authentic a realization of Bach's works
as possible, and by reaffirming the conception of faithful devotion to his work as they understood it, they did
great service. They did not indulge in the subtleties
of argument; they acted. The Bach literature produced by this Youth Movement is unimportant. But
we have the important fruits of their work before
us to-day in a great number of authentic editions of
Bach's works, in the revival of the old instruments, and
in the continuing effort to achieve a reading of the
music which does justice to its real character. Even
though no consolidated conception of Bach himself,
no firm idea of his nature was behind their work,
their simple confession of faith in his work and their
rejection of all the old unauthentic arrangements
cleared the air. Although these young enthusiasts had
gone a few steps farther round the periphery of the
great sun, however, it was evident that they had in

fact not come any closer to it. Nevertheless, through the influence of their efforts Bach's work reached far and wide into circles it would never have touched before. The so-called 'organ-movement' with its return to the acoustic ideals of the Baroque also played its part in the recovery of authentic realizations and the emancipation of Bach's music from the twilight of the Romantics.

Meanwhile, Bach scholars were on the look-out for new foundations in their inquiries. It is characteristic that in the period between the wars not a single comprehensive study of Bach appeared. Efforts were concentrated rather on an immense variety of specialized research, in which scholars were engaged as it were in assembling from all directions, from the historical, the practical, the theoretical, the philosophical, and biographical, the bricks for the building of a new structure. They were collected mainly in the Bach Year Books, edited with such loving devotion by Arnold Schering, and the most valuable achievement of the Neue Bach Gesellschaft. In addition, specific problems were sometimes dealt with in works of comprehensive scholarship. Ernst Kurth undertook a highly important advance into the world of Bach polyphony, Wolfgang Graeser attempted to demonstrate this polyphony as a means of constructive thinking in the *Art of Fugue*, Wilhelm Werker set out to prove the significance of Number and Proportion as the bases of the formal structure of Bach's music, and by so doing opened up a path which other scholars have developed to an appreciation of Bach as the heir of medieval symbolism. Jacques Handschin attempted a philosophical interpretation of the foundations of Bach's music. The question of the sociological bases of Bach's music has not, however, begun to be tackled seriously even to-day. The problem of the religious and dogmatic roots of Bach's art was first dealt with by Hans Besch in 1938. His book is an important first attempt to open up the theological side of Bach's mind and to solve problems which are coming increasingly to the fore in Bach research. The small but admirable study of *Bach in the Age of Rationalism and Early Romanticism*[1] by Gerhard Herz has been almost completely overlooked, as has also the important bibliographical work by Georg Kinsky on *The First Editions of Bach's Works*.[2] One of the most active and fruitful Bach scholars of the twenty years between the wars was the English historian Charles Sanford Terry, who undertook the enormous task of working right through the whole body of documentary material on the life of Bach and made in addition the most thorough-going studies of specific problems, such as the problem of Bach's orchestra, the chorales, and others. As well as a whole series of specialized treatises, he published a

[1] *Bach im Zeitalter des Rationalismus und der Frühromantik.*
[2] *Die Originalausgaben der Werke Bachs.*

first-rate edition of Bach's Cantata texts, arranged liturgically, and a biography which was translated into German, with a preface by Karl Straube, and read by a wide public. Terry did not attempt a new picture of Bach, but apart from the discovery of many fresh details his great merit consists in having described Bach's life with a vividness and a vitality never attained in any previous work. If his exposition does occasionally border on the sensational (as in the 'Battle of the Prefects'), and forgoes any attempt to interpret the mysteries and the deeper background problems of Bach, nevertheless it must still be considered at any rate the liveliest portrayal of his life that we possess. The fact must not be forgotten, of course, that Terry says practically nothing about Bach's works. Only the actual facts of the outward course of his life are the subject of his vivid narrative.

Why did Bach research split up in the years between the wars into the specialist investigation of isolated problems, why was no concentrated and comprehensive study produced, no new and convincing interpretation achieved, why, in spite of the extremely assiduous, honest, and often enthusiastic efforts that were made, did only partial results emerge, with no connecting bond of unity? The reasons were inherent in the whole intellectual and cultural situation of the time and it was not merely Bach research that was affected. Solely in order to complete the record let me mention in passing that the last twelve years produced a crop of grotesquely inaccurate works, written to suit current political ideology by such writers as Willy Pastor, Kurt Rücker, and Karl Rutkowski. Altogether, then, there have been many fresh beginnings and new insights, many useful as well as useless contributions, an immense body of specialized research, but no consolidated picture, no concentrated vision of the man and his achievement as a whole. Is the history of Bach simply to trickle away then in this careless age of general disintegration? May the Bach movement have been after all simply the affair of a band of romantic enthusiasts? Or may the Bach revival still have it in its power to lead us to a far deeper understanding than has ever been achieved so far?

We have not yet reached that stage, for we are still living on the inheritance of the Romantics, in this as in every other field of art and music and cultural life generally. In the meantime, however, the foundation-stones on which a new conception of Bach could be based have been laid in the last thirty years in the unassuming labours of a German scholar, uninfluenced by the passing opinions of the day, by the ideas of critics and journalists, or by political catastrophes. The music scholar Arnold Schering devoted a lifetime to the study of Bach and his age. His published works are scattered and of interest chiefly to fellow specialists. An abundance of new ideas has emerged from his work in which he broached a mass of historical, analytical, aesthetic, and philosophical problems as well as problems of source-criticism. A full-length study of *Bach's Leipzig Church Music*[1] which appeared in 1936 was devoted to specialized source-criticism, but in his last work, published in 1941, the year in which he died, a comprehensive *Musical History of Leipzig in the Age of Bach and Hiller*, he attempted to sum up the whole of the twenty-seven Leipzig years and to draw a picture of Bach's life and character, of his influence and inner spirit, which is of interest to the wider circles of Bach's friends. We owe an enormous amount of fresh detailed information to this ripe fruit of the work of forty years, and even though some of Schering's conclusions must be disputed, there can be no doubt that in this great work German scholarship has once more followed worthily in the steps of Spitta and Schweitzer. Schering was not free, unfortunately, of the Romantic tendency to idealization and he inclined to an idyllic conception of history which sometimes stifled the actual results of his own historical research. A new conception of Bach arose, indeed, but it was not a satisfying conception since historical reality was interpreted from a mildly nostalgic point of view which had been out of date since Terry. In this last work Schering completely failed to touch on the vital problem of the bases of the essential Bach spirit, of Bach's relation to

[1] *Bachs Leipziger Kirchenmusik.*

God and man. He greatly contributed, on the other hand, to our knowledge of Bach's system of musical expression in the many articles which he contributed to the Bach Year Books and in his introductions to new editions of the Cantatas and so on. With great courage Schering attempted a completely new interpretation of Bach's music and with his discovery of Bach's use of symbolism he opened up a new approach to Bach's innermost conception of religion and dogma. Schering was able to show that Bach in his vocal works was not merely aiming, as Schweitzer had thought, at translating the words into the language of musical sound, but, in addition to that, as Dilthey had already surmised intuitively, he was symbolizing in his music the hidden relationships, the ultimate ideas, in fact the 'coincidentia oppositorum' itself, which elude the untutored reader and listener, since to understand them a whole training in the subtleties and sophistications of the old-Lutheran scholasticism is required. This interpretation seems to open a door on the whole world of Bach's innermost conceptions and ideas. To open it still farther must now be one of the most urgent concerns of future Bach research. May not Schering's whole work on Bach be perhaps symbolical of the fact that with the catastrophe of the Second World War the era of specialization has come to an end and the way made clear for a new conception of the whole subject?

A period of nearly 200 years has passed since the death of Bach. By the efforts of 150 years the first weak trickles of Bach's posthumous fame have been gathered into a mighty torrent. The dammed-up waters have been released and an influence of unique proportions secured for his work. His stature has been raised to levels of greatness increasingly beyond the scan of ordinary men. Sebastian Bach through the changes of history is a mirror and symbol of the transformations of history, and the history of Bach has become the history of music itself.

PRINTED IN
GREAT BRITAIN
AT THE
UNIVERSITY PRESS
OXFORD
BY
CHARLES BATEY
PRINTER
TO THE
UNIVERSITY

086516